FERNDOWN
A Pictorial History

Looking west along Wimborne Road, Ferndown, in the 1940s with Creamer's grocery store and Baker's cycle repair shop on the right.

FERNDOWN
A Pictorial History

Audrey Greenhalgh
and
Roger Guttridge

Phillimore

1997

Published by
PHILLIMORE & CO. LTD.,
Shopwyke Manor Barn, Chichester, West Sussex

ISBN 1 86077 038 X

Printed and bound in Great Britain by
BIDDLES LTD.
Guildford, Surrey

List of Illustrations

Frontispiece: Wimborne Road in the 1940s

Acknowledgements

The authors are especially grateful to the following for information, the loan of photographs and permission to reproduce them: Helen and Geoff Tyler, Alan and Vera Dean, Tony Croucher, Simon Rowley, the late Mr. D. Brown, Miss N. Stewart, Harry Ashley, Mark Loader, Terry White, Mr. D. Brown, Mr. H. Bolton, Mrs. R. Matthews, Miss N. Stewart, Ferndown Historical Society, Kitchenhams Ltd. and *The Bournemouth Daily Echo.* They are also particularly grateful to Roger Holman for assistance in copying certain photographs.

Introduction

The Town on the Heath

In 100 years Ferndown has grown from a modest village on the heath into a town boasting the fifth largest population in Dorset and the largest of any non-coastal town. Its expansion has been swift and dramatic, particularly since the Second World War, and has totally transformed the environment. Where 200 years ago smugglers hauled their contraband across deserted acres of heather and gorse, today sprawling housing estates occupy the horizon on all sides. Where 50 years ago there were corner shops whose customers were on first-name terms, today impersonal supermarkets attract shoppers in their thousands. The Edwardian elementary school has given way to a three-tier education system; the humble soccer pavilion to a thriving sports centre; the pre-war village hall competes with a plush modern community centre. Yet within the boundaries of this modern town is a community with character, with history—and with a few surprises up its suburban sleeve.

Prehistoric Ferndown

Evidence of prehistoric occupation at Ferndown is thin, although the heathland itself indicates that Bronze-Age man was in the area around 500 B.C. The heathland which once covered most of South-East Dorset but of which only 15 per cent now remains was inadvertently created by Bronze-Age farmers whose clearance of prehistoric woodland led to the leaching of nutrients from the sandy and highly porous soil.

The third edition of John Hutchins' *History of Dorset* records an archaeological discovery 'in this parish' in 1847, when a barrow was opened under the direction of Sir John Guest and in it was found 'an urn of the rudest pottery, formed of sun-burnt clay of dark brown colour, but too much broken to convey an accurate idea of either its size or shape'. The contents of the urn presented evidence of calcined bones. In addition, arrowheads, scrapers and a Neolithic skull have been found at Longham which, like Hampreston village, Stapehill, Tricketts Cross and Ferndown itself, forms part of the large and historic civil and ecclesiastical parish of Hampreston. A few yards outside the parish boundary, in the neighbouring parish of West Parley, is the prehistoric hillfort of Dudsbury, which was excavated by the well-known local archaeologist, artist and writer Heywood Sumner in 1921. Before the excavation, Sumner suspected that the site had been occupied well before the time of the Roman invasion. In the event, the dig proved it was no older than Iron Age, although this in itself was a worthwhile discovery at a time when the dates of most hillforts were unproven.

'Wooded Hill, Ferny Place'

The population of Ferndown remained sparse or non-existent until relatively modern times. The earliest documentary evidence of its existence as an identifiable location dates from the 14th century, when it was referred to as 'Fyrne' (1321) and 'Ferne' (1358). This part of the name Ferndown derives from one of two Old English words— 'fergen', meaning wooded hill, or 'fierne', meaning ferny place. Both are equally possible—central Ferndown does occupy a small hill, known today as Penny's Hill, in the midst of an otherwise fairly flat area between Uddens Water and the River Stour; but the nature of the soil and vegetation hereabouts are consistent with it also having been a 'ferny place' before farming and development changed the landscape beyond recognition. The second syllable of Ferndown comes from the old word 'dun', meaning hill or down, and was acquired later.

The Mother Community

With Ferndown itself attracting so little human activity until modern times, the greatest attention in the past was naturally bestowed on the 'mother community' of Hampreston. This is referred to as Hame in the Domesday Survey of 1086, Hamme in 1204, Hamme Preston in 1244 and Hamepreston in 1299. Hamm in Old English means the enclosure or river meadow (the village occupies the east bank of the River Stour); Preston means priest farm or estate, from the Old English preost and tun, probably an allusion to lands here belonging to the College of Wimborne Minster.

Domesday Book identifies four landholders in the manor of Hampreston in 1086, suggesting that there were at least four settlements there in Norman times. King William I himself was one landholder; the others were Aiulf the Chamberlain, William Chernet (who held it from the wife of Hugh the son of Grip) and Thorkell, a thane or member of the King's household. In the case of Thorkell's holding, we are told that 'the Queen gave this land to Azelin; now the King has it in lordship'. Hampreston landholders before the Norman Conquest in 1066 are identified as Saul and Aldwin.

The laity tax, or lay subsidy, of 1327 lists 32 taxpayers at Hampreston and the equivalent record for 1332 names an identical number. Of these, the richest in 1332 were Robert Lacy, who was assessed to pay tax of 4s. 10d., and Robert Bercario (4s. 8d.). Sixteenth-century records show the Kings and Biddlecombes as the dominant families. Of 26 people assessed to pay the lay tax in 1525, Thomas Kyng was the wealthiest with taxable goods worth £25, followed by [.....?] Byttylcombe (£20) and John Byttlycon (£14). By the time of the 1545 assessment, Richard Byddelcomb was the richest of Hampreston's 20 taxpayers with goods worth £18, followed by John Hancocke (£16) and Richard Byddelcomb (£13).

The same families feature prominently in the muster rolls of 1539, a record of all able men aged between 16 and 60 in King Henry VIII's kingdom who held weapons. The list, one of several compiled nationally in the 16th century, was commissioned at a time when invasion by France was feared. It was intended as an assessment of the men, weapons and equipment available to the king. In the case of Hampreston, the 1539 roll lists 39 individuals of whom 15 are identified as 'able archers' and nine as 'able billmen'. The record also reveals that the tithing of Hampreston 'hath a whole complete harness', or suit of armour, while Thomas Kyng had a 'complete harness for a bowman' but was 'not able' himself, Hugh Bettylcombe had a 'whole harness', Richard Bettylcombe a bow, 12 arrows and a 'whole harness' and William Hancocke senior (also unable) half a harness, which probably consisted only of a breastplate. John Bemyster and William Benet both had swords, Thomas

Pers had a bow and 12 'of the parish's arrows' and William Roke had a bill belonging to his master Hugh Bettylcombe. Most of the remaining men had a bill or a bow (in a few cases with four, six or 12 arrows). William Michell had a bow, a billet and a sallet, or short brimmed helmet; John Byrte also had a sallet as well as his bill.

Dust to Dust

Traditionally the people of Hampreston looked to the nearby market town of Wimborne for most of their commercial needs, and to some extent for their spiritual needs, since the church was originally a chapel of Wimborne Minster. In the Middle Ages, they even had to make their last earthly journeys to Wimborne, as there was no burial ground at Hampreston. The distance was only two miles but the journey could present a major challenge in wet weather, when the road became 'muddy and deep and commonly flooded by the River Stour, so that four or five days together pedestrians cannot pass there'. As a result, it was claimed in 1440, 'corpses are kept so long above the ground that men abhor to bury them or to pass with them to the place of burial'!

Eventually Hampreston got its burial ground, in the churchyard of All Saints' Church, a building whose tower and chancel date from the 14th century but which was substantially rebuilt in the 1890s. Those who benefited from the belated burial arrangements included Miles Bownes, 'sometime Rector of this church', who was laid to rest on 6 September 1630 and had a quaint monument erected in his memory. It includes the roughly-hewn effigy of a clergyman in black gown and ruff with a Bible open before him and an inscription underneath which also mentions his eight children by name. Other memorials inside the church are dedicated to the Greathead family, who were patrons of the church following their purchase of Uddens House from Nathaniel Gundry in 1790.

'An Infamous Heretic'

Hampreston's parish register dates from 1617 and contains one particularly unusual entry recording the excommunication by the Pope of Henry Goldney, of Hampreston, 'an infamous heretic', for 'the heinous crime of sacrilege with the images of our Holy Saints', for 'forsaking our most holy religion' and for continuing in 'heresy, blasphemy and corrupt lust'. The papal declaration, pronounced by the priest at Stapehill in 1758, condemns Goldney to be 'buffeted, scourged and spitted upon'.

The parish accounts for Hampreston record payments to 'travelling women, near their time', which may not have been as charitable as it sounds, as the true objective was to remove them from the parish before their children were born so that they did not become a burden in the future. Some were less than co-operative—one woman, in 1715, cost the parish 9s. 6d. 'paid to officers to convey her away'! The following year a payment of 1s. 6d. was made for 'conveying a dying soldier away out of the parish'. More generous, perhaps, were the payments in 1758 of 2s. 6d. to each of 'several persons that lately came from the Inquisition who was very objects of pity'. In 1720 and 1721, the parish paid out for prayer books purchased 'to avert the plague'; in 1745 for 'a prayer book against the [Jacobite] Rebellion'; and in 1779 'against invasion'. In 1761, the churchwardens noted payments of 2s. 6d. to 'the ringers to spend on the day

King George III was crowned'. A common feature of the accounts in Hampreston, as in many other parishes, is the rewards paid to people (often children) who caught birds and animals regarded as vermin. Sparrowheads were paid for by the dozen (2d. a dozen was a typical rate): in 1733 the vermin-hunters brought in a record 272 dozen! The heads of foxes, otters and badgers were worth 1s. each, polecats 6d., stoats and hedge-hogs 4d. and rats 1d.

The Smugglers' Heath

In the 18th and early 19th centuries, Ferndown had only three industries of note—agriculture, horticulture and smuggling. In the case of smuggling, the particular geography of the area made an involvement in what was then a thriving illicit trade inevitable. A few miles to the south were the gently-sloping sandy beaches of Poole and Bourne, where huge quantities of spirits, wine, tea and tobacco were regularly brought ashore to be transported across the uninhabited Bourne Heath (now Bournemouth) and beyond. The nearby harbour towns of Poole and Christchurch were home to many a smuggling ship and many a smuggling gang; and the village of Kinson, just across the River Stour from Longham, was a major smuggling centre for decades.

There are several clues to Ferndown's past involvement in smuggling, including the comments of a 19th-century rector of Hampreston. In furtherance of his attempts to persuade the church authorities to open a day school in the village, he wrote that 'the parishioners are chiefly poor but formerly prosperous, when smuggling was much in practice'. At Tricketts Cross today, we find the *Smugglers' Haunt* pub and restaurant and, in nearby Wimborne Road, a tea-room and guest house called Smuggler's Cottage. The *Smugglers' Haunt*, which has twice burnt down and been rebuilt since the Second World War, has no direct connection with smuggling, since it was not built until the present century, although there was at one time a much older cottage in the grounds. The thatched Smuggler's Cottage, however, probably does have a genuine smuggling pedigree, since it is not only the oldest building in Ferndown (parts of it are said to date back 400 years) but was one of very few buildings close to a known smuggling route from the coast across Ferndown to West Moors and beyond. By an unfortunate co-incidence, this cottage too was badly damaged by fire in the 1980s and subsequently repaired. The lane which adjoins the cottage is traditionally known as Smuggler's Lane and leads towards West Moors.

One of England's best-known smugglers, Isaac Gulliver, who became a wealthy man through the contraband trade, has strong connections with Ferndown. Though born in Wiltshire in 1745, he spent most of his adult life in Dorset and moved to Longham in 1778. Until recently the only Longham building which could be indisputably linked to him was the *White Hart Inn*, which was mentioned in a newspaper advertisement as the venue for an auction to be held on 12 April 1779 for the sale of '20 good hack horses, the property of Isaac Gulliver, of the same place'. Some writers have taken the phrase 'of the same place' to imply that Gulliver actually lived at the *White Hart*. This is not beyond the bounds of possibility, since he did keep an inn at Thorney Down, near Sixpenny Handley, before moving to Longham. However, as recently as the summer of 1996 a document came to light which firmly links the smuggler with another surviving building in the village, Hillamsland Farm in Christchurch Road, now owned by Dudsbury

Golf Club, whose course adjoins it. In this document, dated 1812, labourer William Lockyer, then aged about 45, makes a sworn statement about his previous places of residence. He states that he was born at Kinson and that when he was about 15 he 'went to service and lived two years as a yearly servant with Mr Isaac Gulliver of Hillam Lands in that part of the parish of Hampreston that lies in the county of Hants'. This would have been about 1782, possibly a little earlier or later, if Lockyer's estimate of his age was inaccurate, which is possible. Interestingly, the Jacobean Hillamsland Farmhouse still has a huge cellar underneath it; there is also said to be a tunnel leading from it towards the cottages at Dudsbury.

By 1783, Isaac Gulliver was living at Kinson, just across the River Stour from Longham, and describing himself as a wine merchant. In 1789, however, he gave his address as West Moors, where his property is still known as Gulliver's Farm. It is quite extraordinary that, like Smuggler's Cottage and the *Smugglers' Haunt*, this too has been rebuilt since the Second World War after suffering severe fire damage. Gulliver— once described by the Collector of Customs at Poole as 'a man of great speculating genius'—ended his days at Wimborne, where he died in 1822 leaving bequests worth £60,000 and property in four counties!

Answers in the Soil

While smuggling provided a useful income supplement for many members of the labouring classes (a labourer could earn as much from a night's tub running as he could from a week on the land), it was still agriculture which dominated the working lives of most local people, as it did in most rural areas. There were a few farms and smallholdings, especially in the fertile land closest to the River Stour and Uddens Water. But there were also large areas of the parish, particularly the area around the present-day centre of Ferndown, which remained uncultivated. The earliest Ordnance Survey map of the area, published in 1811, shows most of the area between Hampreston village and the River Avon south of Ringwood as heath and common land. Within this tract of land several different areas are identified by name, among them Hampreston Heath, which includes the Ferndown Common and town centre of today, Parley Common, Hurn (spelt Hern) Common and, between West Moors and St Leonards, Woolbridge Heath. The same map also shows two sizeable forestry plantations, the smaller one at Uddens and Whitesheet to the north of Hampreston Heath, the larger one at St Leonards, St Ives and Matchams, to the north of the present-day Bournemouth International Airport.

An offshoot of agriculture was horticulture and, if anything has a longstanding tradition in Ferndown, it is market gardening. Stewart's, the company with the most remarkable record in this field, claim a plant-growing pedigree dating back to Forfarshire in 1742. In 1864, David and William Stewart put down new roots in Dorset, acquiring a 74-acre nursery site on the corner of Wimborne Road and West Moors Road, where the business remained for almost exactly 100 years. In 1953 they converted a number of potting sheds to form what is claimed to have been the first garden centre in the UK. A second centre was opened at Christchurch and today the family business survives there and a few miles from Ferndown in the neighbouring parish of Holt. Another long-established business is Rosina Nurseries, started near the corner of Church and Ringwood Roads by Frank and Rosina Froud at some time before 1891. The family still run it, although part of the nursery was lost to a compulsory purchase order in 1982 and is now occupied by part of the Ferndown Centre car park. Haskins' garden centre, another business with pre-20th-century roots, arrived at Tricketts Cross in the early 1960s, moved to Longham in 1994 and is now the biggest of several horticultural businesses in the parish.

Ferndown becomes a Village

It was during the 19th century that Ferndown grew from a few scattered cottages on the heath into a village in its own right. In the national census of 1801, the parish of Hampreston is shown as having 133 houses and a population of 683, of whom 387 were females. By 1891, the number of houses had grown to 357 and the number of inhabitants to 1,608, of whom 846 were females and only 762 were males. A large proportion of this growth occurred at Ferndown rather than at Longham, Hampreston and Stapehill, which between them had previously accounted for the vast majority of the population. The 1891 census also records five pubs, four of them (*Pitman's Beerhouse*, the *King's Arms*, the *White Hart* and the *Angel Inn*) at Longham. Longham also had a *Coffee Tavern*, kept by 80-year-old widow Ann Martin, while the fifth pub recorded was the *Pure Drop Inn* at Ferndown. Interestingly, all but *Pitman's Beerhouse* and the *Coffee Tavern* have survived to this day.

The Holy Cross Abbey

The significantly larger number of females in the census returns is partly explained by the existence of a Cistercian nunnery at Stapehill, which opened in 1802 and closed in 1989. The first Mother Superior was Madame de Chabannes who, a few years earlier, during the French Revolution, was in a Paris prison cell awaiting the guillotine. She and a number of other nuns apparently survived only because the dreaded Robespierre was overthrown. They went into exile, travelling through Switzerland, Germany, Austria, Poland and Russia before finally arriving in London in 1801. The following year the 8th Lord Arundel of Wardour generously donated a site at Stapehill and in October 1802 Madame de Chabannes moved in along with eight other nuns, five of them novices. The nuns are reputed to have lived in great poverty in the early years and to have toiled ceaselessly to bring the barren heathland under cultivation. Their labour included drainage work on the low-lying land and land clearance using pickaxes. A local farmer was paid 10 guineas a year to advise the nuns on cultivation. Madame de Chabannes herself used to fill carts with manure between 4 and 5 in the morning ready for collection at 6 a.m. The nuns received support from a community of Cistercian monks at Lulworth, Dorset, who made shoes for them and sent over barrels of milk and later a cow so that they could produce their own. In return the nuns washed and mended the altar linen from Lulworth Monastery, which also supplied the nuns' first confessor, Père Antoine, and his successors.

The Stapehill nuns received a major setback in 1818 when fire destroyed much of the complex. Legend has it that the Reverend Mother threw a relic of the true cross into the flames, at which point they began to subside. The relic was found, unbroken, under the ashes some days later. The fire happened on 3 May, the date of the nuns' patronal festival marking the Intervention of the Holy Cross. The damaged buildings were rebuilt and extended. The 1891 census lists 43 nuns, of whom 33 were born in Ireland, one in France, one in New Zealand and the remaining eight in Great Britain.

Only one was born in Dorset—Monica Rolls, aged 49, a native of Lulworth. In 1927 the community became the Holy Cross Abbey and the status of Abbess was conferred on the Prioress. In recent decades, however, membership of the community declined to the point that there were too few nuns to manage the property. In 1989 it was sold and the nuns moved to a new home at Whitland, South Wales. The premises reopened in 1992 as Stapehill Abbey, a popular tourist attraction featuring local history, crafts and gardens.

By Rail and Road

A crucial factor in the development of Victorian Ferndown was the arrival of the railway. The line from Southampton to Dorchester, opened in 1847, skirted along the northern edge of Ferndown, passing through West Moors, Uddens and Stapehill on its way to Wimborne. The line was known as Castleman's Corkscrew after its main promoter, Wimborne solicitor Charles Castleman, and on account of its meandering route. However, it was another 20 years before Ferndown acquired the use of a station closer than Wimborne or Ringwood. The change resulted from the opening in 1867 of an additional line running south-west from Salisbury via Downton, Breamore, Fordingbridge and Verwood to join the Southampton to Dorchester line at West Moors. The station was sited at West Moors, a little to the south-west of the junction, and travellers were made aware by the platform signs that they had arrived at 'West Moors for Ferndown'.

If the railway assisted Ferndown's development as a village, it was another transport facility which greatly aided its expansion to the status of a town. This was the bridge across the River Stour in New Road, West Parley, a project instigated by local landowners Lady Wimborne and Lt. Col. C.R. Prideaux-Brune. The first Ensbury Bridge, as it was known before acquiring its present name of New Road Bridge, was built in 1910 but collapsed a few years later and was replaced in 1923 by the present iron structure. This provided both Ferndown and Parley with a more direct route into Bournemouth—a route which in the last century had been served only by a rope ferry and later a punt between Ensbury and Parley.

The Trappings of Growth

As Ferndown grew, the public facilities naturally grew with it and increasingly it took on the persona of a self-contained village rather than the mere collection of scattered cottages it had previously been. Kelly's *Directory* of 1911 lists a number of traders and professional people who between them provided for most of the community's essential day-to-day needs. They included Police Constable Herbert Vacher, baker Jess Bracher, publican Fred Ellis at the *Pure Drop*, grocers Harry Galton and A.G.Whittenham, butcher Reuben Webb, cycle agent Ernest Goswell, schoolmistress Mrs. Teresa Trevett and laundress Mrs. Emma Penny. It was Mrs. Penny who gave her name to the area around the crossroads at the centre of Ferndown, which to this day is known as Penny's Hill. By 1920, G. Robertson of Longham was advertising motor char-a-banc trips to the Derby and other events in the 'Ferndown Rambler'. Departure time from Wimborne was 6.30 a.m. and the return fare was £1 1s.

The first Anglican church at Ferndown (as distinct from Hampreston) appeared in the late 19th century and was a relatively modest building seating only 50 people. As Ferndown expanded, however, the first St Mary's Church became increasingly inadequate for the community it served. In about 1930 a site on the corner of Church Road and Ringwood Road was earmarked for a replacement building but there was also talk of an alternative plan to build a pub on the plot. Fearful of the latter idea, Mrs. M.A. Lyon, who lived opposite and was a devout churchgoer, bought the land from the Wilcox family and donated it to the church authorities. She also stipulated that there should be no burials in the church grounds, which is why there are no gravestones there today. The church was begun in 1933 and opened the following year, although the tower was not added until 1971-2.

Ferndown's first Congregational Church, which stood in Victoria Road at the corner of what is now Westwood Avenue, was destroyed by fire in 1905 and replaced by the present United Reformed Church in Wimborne Road. Other early Ferndown churches included a Primitive Methodist Church in Wimborne Road and a Methodist Church which occupied the building now used as the Ferndown Fire Station.

The earlier St Mary's Church building also served as an infants school until the opening of the Ferndown Council School in Church Road during the First World War. It was run virtually single-handed by Mrs. Teresa Trevett, known as 'Governess' Trevett, whose pupils stayed until the age of seven, at which point they had to walk to Hampreston or West Moors to continue their education. The Ferndown Elementary School opened in 1901 with 30 or 40 pupils but numbers steadily rose as Ferndown's population grew. By 1911 there were more than 70 names on the roll and in 1915, when the council school opened in two buildings and began accepting older pupils, the number admitted was 162 pupils. Surviving records of the school include the punishment book for 1934, when caning was still a regular occurrence. Typical offences include disobedience, insolence, defiance and stone throwing, which usually warranted one or two strokes on the hand. Wilfred Rossiter and Leonard Baily committed a more spectacular crime in 1934 and received one stroke of the cane each for 'lighting fire-works in school bus'.

Ferndown's growth also brought public services, including mains water in the late 19th century, gas in 1911, telephones in the same era and electricity a few years later. The village still had little industry at this time, although a brickworks operated success-fully from the early 1920s until 1963 using locally-quarried clay. The site was sold in 1966 to become the Ferndown Industrial Estate, leaving Brickyard Lane, which runs roughly parallel to the main industrial road, as the only reminder of the former use.

Ferndown, like virtually every other UK community, suffered its share of losses during the two world wars. The First World War claimed the lives of 48 men from the parish, the Second World War 25 lives. Several families lost two or three men and the Hart family lost five in the course of the two wars.

Leisure and Tourism

Leisure and tourism have played a part in Ferndown's 20th-century history, with a zoo, a nudist colony, a major golf course and several hotels listed among its past or present attractions. The nudist colony was in West Moors Road but it was the Ferndown Zoo which generated the most attention in the early 1950s, both locally and nationally. The zoo was opened by Mrs. Dorothy Sadler in 1947 on a site opposite Heath Farm (now Heath Farm Road and Way) and Tice's Ferndown Duck Farm in Ringwood Road, said to be the largest in Europe with 20,000 ducks whose feathers were supplied to the makers of pillows and bedding. Mrs. Sadler's enterprise began as a pet's corner but her collection of animals became increasingly exotic and by 1952 included bears, leopards, a gorilla and a lion called Ajax, who became Ferndown's most famous inhabitant and its noisiest. Former Ferndown trader Alan Dean, who lived nearby, recalls that Ajax's roaring reached a climax between lunchtime each Friday and 10 a.m. the following day. This followed the administration of worming cake to Ajax at 10 a.m. each Friday, after which he would be starved by Mrs. Sadler for 24 hours and would express his protests in the only way he could!

The zoo proved a great attraction each holiday season with about 10,000 visitors a year passing through its gates. It was rather less popular with many of the locals, however, who were not only disturbed by Ajax's roaring but feared that the king of the jungle might escape. Their fears were understandable, as several other animals, including two Himalayan black bears called Rupert and Mary, had already escaped and been recaptured. After much protest and debate, including a public inquiry, Mrs. Sadler was ordered by the Ministry of Housing to close the zoo. Many of the animals went to Chessington Zoo but all attempts to place Ajax, Rupert and Mary failed until 5 December 1955, when their plight was featured on the BBC Television programme Panorama, as a result of which offers of new homes flooded in. In the end all three remaining animals were accepted by Butlin's holiday camp at Skegness. The site of Ferndown Zoo is now occupied by Longacre Drive.

Ferndown Golf Course, opened in 1922, has long been a magnet to visitors and has staged many major tournaments, including the Hennessy Cup in 1982 and 1984, the European Professional Ladies Open in 1987 and the British Ladies Open in 1989. The course is also associated with the well-known Percy Alliss, who was the club professional before the war, and his television commentator son, Peter, who was brought up in Ferndown.

The golf club, together with the proximity of the New Forest, Bournemouth, Poole and other tourist attractions, have combined to foster a notable hotel industry in Ferndown, where the main hotels today are the *Dormy* and the *Coach House*. The *Coach House* at Tricketts Cross first opened as the *Links Hotel* in about 1930, when it was advertised as having 'good accommodation for golfers'. It became the *Green Parrot*—'the roadhouse on the A31 highway'—in about 1955 before being demolished in 1968 to reopen in 1972 as the *Coach House*, which it remains. The four-star *Dormy*—formerly a nursing home and a convalescent home for Second World War airmen—was opened as a 35-bedroom hotel by a Bournemouth mayoress soon after the war and has since grown into a prestige establishment with 120 bedrooms, a plush leisure centre and a clientèle which includes many of England's Premier and First Division football clubs, publishing and record companies and even the pop group Take That!

From Village to Town

In the 1950s Ferndown could still be accurately described as a village but there were already hints of the expansion to come. Post-war development of the Tricketts Cross housing estate was following in the late 1950s by the sale of Mark Brown's farmland between Church and Victoria Roads to become Ferndown's first private housing estate. Other major developments followed, including the Dare estate in the late 1960s and an estate off Ameysford Road soon after. Main drainage arrived in 1962. The population grew rapidly, from 3,000 in 1951 to 16,000 in 1991. The 1960s also saw the beginnings of the Ferndown Industrial Estate, now one of the biggest in the area, as well as construction of the Ferndown Upper School and a new youth centre. Ferndown Sports Centre was the main addition of the early 1970s while 1977 saw Ferndown promoted to the civic status of a town with its own town (as opposed to parish) council and a mayor rather than a plain chairman (the first mayor of Ferndown was Robin Spencer who, by virtue of his birth in Dudsbury Avenue in 1924, was in a small minority of genuine natives!).

The 1980s produced the Tesco superstore in the town centre together with a row of additional shops, a new public library, community centre and day centre, some of which were provided at Tesco's expense as part of the planning deal. The Tesco scheme, designed to give Ferndown the 'heart' or coherent town centre it previously lacked, was highly controversial at the time but appears to have fulfilled its objective to a large extent. The Ferndown by-pass also appeared in 1985, removing at least some of the enormous traffic pressure from Ferndown, which until that time was bisected by two A-class roads. The 1990s have also brought change, including the demolition of the old Ferndown First School (originally the Council School) in Church Road, and construction of another major supermarket, Sainsbury's at Tricketts Cross, whose appearance has once again shifted the balance of trading power in Ferndown.

Shopping in Ferndown

1 A.C. Whittenham's Central Stores in Wimborne Road, Ferndown, in the 1920s. The shop was sited between the junctions with Victoria Road and Church Road. Mr. Whittenham, who boasted the unusual name of 'Antwerp', also hired out a pony and trap from his premises.

2 Galton's Cash Supply Stores and Post Office at the corner of Wimborne Road and Victoria Road, Ferndown. A small section of the adjoining Primitive Methodist Chapel can be seen on the left complete with a poster advertising the Whit Monday fête.

3 Ferndown Post Office and Stores in the mid-1920s. The Post Office and nearby garage were run by Mrs. Galton. The clutter of signs outside includes a large board directing people to Ferndown Golf Club. There had been a makeshift café opposite the Post Office, but this appears to have made way for the beginnings of Queens Road.

4 The Ferndown Post Office Stores in 1942. Note the pre-war telephone kiosk and the advertisement for the shop's Circulating Library.

5 Wimborne Road, Ferndown, looking towards the junction with Church Road in the 1960s. The shops include the Kingsland Cycle Works (far left), the Milborne Stores, which had a circulating library, and the Ferndown Stores.

6 The proud boast of this little hut was that it housed Ferndown's first fish and chip shop! That was in the 1930s, before Mr. and Mrs. Arthur Wareham moved their business from this site at the corner of Wimborne Road and Queens Road to more permanent premises in Victoria Road. When this picture was taken in the 1920s, the hut housed a barber's shop run by F.G. Prior, whose name can just be made out above the window. A poster inside the rear wall of the shop is advertising a village dance!

7 *Left.* Frank Fey's butcher's shop, which opened in Wimborne Road in 1926. Products advertised on the hoarding to the left include quality English and chilled beef, pork, Canterbury lamb, poultry and rabbits. The billboards to the right are for the Plaza Cinema (which was showing *The Merry Widow*) and the Regent, both of which would have been in either Bournemouth or Poole.

8 *Below left.* The same shop in the 1950s, by now enlarged and owned by M.J. Pitt, 'high class butcher'.

9 *Below.* Reuben Webb's butcher's shop in Ringwood Road, Ferndown, at the turn of the century. The business, established in 1895, passed through three generations of the Webb family. The *White Heather* pub now occupies the site.

10 Charlie the RAC man was a familiar sight on traffic duty at Penny's Hill, seen here in 1936. The shops on the corner of Ringwood Road and Victoria Road included Reg Turner's pharmacy (although the canopy says W.P. Arnott) and John Maidment's tailor's shop.

11 The additional telephone lines on the nearest pole suggest this is a slightly later picture, again showing Turner's the chemists on the corner. Destinations listed on the direction sign include Bournemouth and Christchurch (left) and Wimborne, West Moors and Verwood (right).

12 Post-war Penny's Hill, looking towards Tricketts Cross, shows Jolliffe and Son's furnishing business (far left).

13 Penny's Hill in the 1950s, looking towards Victoria Road.

14 *Above left*. Ferndown's first pet shop, opened in Ringwood Road by Alan and Vera Dean in 1954 and since demolished. The site is now occupied by a modern parade of shops including a cycle shop, butcher's and off-licence.

15 *Left*. The swinging '60s finds Ferndown boasting a new parade of shops in Ringwood Road.

16 *Above*. Longham Post Office, seen on the left in this pre-Second World War photograph, and on the other side of the turning to Ham Lane is the Congregational Church.

17 A post-Second World War view of Longham showing the Post Office and General Stores on the right, the *White Hart* on the left and the Congregational Church.

18 J. and C. Vigis's drapery store at Longham, *c*.1920. The cottage next door on the right was the police house.

19 Kitchenham's aerial view of Ferndown in 1982, before the construction of the Tesco superstore and adjoining shops, public library and the Ferndown Centre. The crossroads at Penny's Hill are on the extreme right of the picture with Victoria Road running to the top of the picture and Ringwood Road to the bottom.

20 Another Kitchenham's shot, this time showing Ferndown in 1986 after the appearance of Tesco and associated buildings. Penny's Hill is at the bottom centre of the picture with the first and middle schools, youth centre and playing fields at the top.

Hotels and Hostelries

21 'Teas & refreshments always ready' boasts the sign outside the *Country Hotel* on the right of this picture of Penny's Hill, *c.*1920. It later became Webb's butcher's shop and, later still, a Strong's off-licence owned by Mr. and Mrs. Alex Nelmes.

22 The original *Pure Drop* in Wimborne Road, Ferndown, in the 1920s. The lettering on the highest of the gables tells us it was an Eldridge Pope pub.

23 The old *Pure Drop* was subsequently rebuilt and reopened as *The Ferndown Hotel*, pictured here *c*.1960. In recent years it has reverted to its earlier name of *The Pure Drop*.

24 The *Whincroft Hotel* in Wimborne Road, Ferndown, pictured in its pre-war days as a private house, called simply Whincroft. It was built in 1894-5 by David Charles Stewart on one of 65 plots of land sold by the Ferndown Estate. Stewart's initials appear on an engraved stone and his Scottish ancestry clearly influenced his choice of name—'Whin' is a Scottish word for gorse or furze and 'Croft' is a crofter's smallholding. Commander Gordon A. Matthew owned Whincroft from 1924 until his death in 1947. It became a guest house and private hotel in 1948 and has been a pub and restaurant since the mid-1950s.

25 The *Links Hotel* at Tricketts Cross, *c.*1935, when it was advertised as having 'good accommodation for golfers'. It became the *Green Parrot*—'the roadhouse on the A31 highway'—in the mid-1950s and was demolished in 1968 and rebuilt to become the *Coach House Inn*, *c.*1972.

26 Looking across the Tricketts Cross roundabout *c.*1964, towards the *Green Parrot*.

27 An early view of the four-star *Dormy Hotel*, which started life as four houses, three of which were linked before the Second World War to become a nursing home, and then during the war became a convalescent home for airmen. A mayoress of Bournemouth opened it as a 35-bedroom hotel after the war. It now has 120 bedrooms and is regularly used by top football teams, record companies and other prestigious clientèle.

28 The *Innisfail Hotel* at the corner of New Road and Dudsbury Avenue, Ferndown, was owned by Mrs. Marjorie Shipp and was a popular venue for wedding receptions and other family occasions in the 1940s and '50s. It was also used by estate agents for house auctions and in the early 1960s, when Mr. and Mrs. White were the proprietors, provided courts for the newly-formed tennis section of Ferndown Sports Club. It has since been demolished.

29 The end of the road for Alex Nelmes' off-licence in Ringwood Road, Ferndown, seen here under demolition in 1964. It was previously a butcher's shop owned by the Webb family but the site is now occupied by the *White Heather* pub.

30 The *Angel Inn* at Longham in the 1930s. Some older residents remember when this pub had no bar counter and drinks were simply brought in to customers on a tray.

31 *Left*. Ringwood Road, Longham, in the 1920s showing the *White Hart Inn* right of centre. The large white sign advertises 'Hall & Woodhouse celebrated ales and stout, wines and spirits'. This was the pub where the smuggler Isaac Gulliver advertised an auction of his '20 good hack horses' in 1779.

32 *Below left*. Longham at the turn of the century looking towards the *King's Arms* pub. A couple of traction engines can just be made out in the distance. Closer to the camera is a terrace of three gabled houses with a tree outside, of which the middle one was the village police house.

33 *Below*. The *Bridge House Hotel* at Longham in the 1920s. Its location beside the River Stour made it a popular spot among fishermen, including the lady angler in the picture. Others simply enjoyed afternoon teas on the riverbank.

34 The Stour and cottages at Longham, *c.*1950, including the Bridge House, which has since grown into a major hotel and restaurant.

35 The Old Thatch at Uddens Cross in its first incarnation as The Lodge to Uddens House.

36 A rethatched and greatly extended Uddens Lodge in its post-war years as The Old Thatch Tea Cottage. It was damaged by fire in the 1950s and rebuilt to reopen as a pub and restaurant. The Old Thatch—refurbished and rethatched again early in 1997—has an enduring reputation for poltergeist activity with several former licensees and bar staff claiming to have encountered ghostly goings on.

Ferndown at Work

37 Harry Ashley's unique photograph of nuns haymaking at the Holy Cross Abbey, Stapehill, *c.*1939.

38 *Left*. Before the combine harvester or even the lawn mower—Mr. and Mrs. Lowman at work in the orchard behind their home in Princess Road, Ferndown.

39 *Above*. Haymaking was a family affair at the turn of the century, with men, women and children all pitching in to lend a hand while the fine weather lasted. These particular haymakers, pictured in a field in Wimborne Road, Ferndown, are the Wilcox family.

40 *Below*. More people making hay while the sun shone, this time on Farmer Brown's farm at Canford Bottom.

41 A welcome break from haymaking on Mark Brown's farm in Wimborne Road, Ferndown. The men are Mark Brown himself, Maurice Wilcox, Syd Dean, Syd Kensington and George Thorne.

42 An aerial shot of Stewart's Nurseries, taken when their telephone number was Ferndown 5. In the bottom left-hand corner of the picture is the junction of West Moors Road and Wimborne Road.

43 Watering the plants at Stewart's Nurseries in the 1930s.

44 Former potting sheds at Stewart's following their conversion to the first garden centre and shop in 1953.

45 *Above*. Longham Mill, which has actually been Longham pumping station since 1883. The 70ft. tower was demolished in 1924.

46 *Left*. Rick-making for victory in a Hampreston hayfield in 1942.

47 The site of a humble brickworks has given way since the 1960s to the vast industrial sprawl of the Ferndown Industrial Estate, here pictured by Kitchenham's in 1985 during construction of the Ferndown by-pass, which crosses the top of the picture, bisecting the Uddens Plantation.

Ferndown at Play

48 Britannia rules as Ferndown children represent the nations of the British Empire. The occasion was probably a celebration of Empire Day at some time before the First World War.

49 The Ferndown Band, *c.*1903, when moustaches were well in fashion and were sported by 10 of the 15 musicians!

50 A scene from the Longham Fête and Gymkhana in the 1920s.

51 Members of a Ferndown drama group perform a scene from one of their productions. The date is unknown but is thought to predate the formation of Ferndown Sports Club's drama section in 1962. Ferndown has a strong tradition in amateur dramatics and for many years has hosted a drama festival, attracting performers from a wide area.

52 A podgy pair of Humpty Dumpties sit on the wall outside Strong's off-licence at Penny's Hill to advertise the Ferndown Youth Club pantomime in February 1962. The off-licence has since been replaced by the *White Heather* pub.

53 The 1st Ferndown Boy Scouts, *c.*1925.

54 The 1st Hampreston Scouts pictured before setting off for camp in 1935. In the background in Ringwood Road is the cake shop run by scoutmaster Doug Gabe's landlady, Mrs. Martin.

55 Members of the Holt British Legion and Ferndown Social Club A teams pictured at Ferndown Village Hall in 1936 after finishing first and second respectively in the Holt and District Air Rifle League. Presenting the cup (far left) is Mr. O.B.P. Burdon, J.P.

56 The Pure Drop football team pictured outside the pub in the 1920s.

57 The Ferndown School football team 1947-8. The masters are Wilf Houghton (*left*) and Mr. Atwell. Team members, where known, are (*back row, left to right*) Mike Hanham, Jim Scutt, Vic Randall, John King, ...? and (*front*) Ray Feltham, ...?, Geoff Lissenburgh, Don Trickett, Peter Ayling, Ponchie Blake.

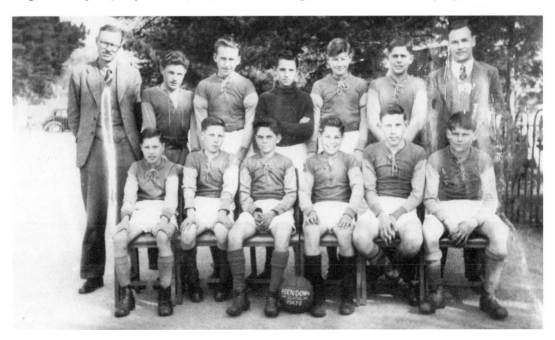

58 Ferndown's football team in the early 1950s. They are (*back row, left to right*) Bill King, Bert Tubbs, Albert Hawker, Bob King, Eric Hames, Billy Mills and (*front row*) Ray Lloyd, Alan Randall, Ray Gilbert, Len Hawker and Pat Joyce.

59 *Above left*. Dorothy Sadler and friends feeding Rupert and Mary, the Himalayan black bears at Ferndown Zoo in 1955, the year of its closure. The bears were among the animals which managed to escape, raising fears about public safety.

60 *Above right*. Ajax the lion, whose presence at Ferndown Zoo was a major factor in the public pressure which led to its closure. As well as fears that he might escape, there was also the question of his incessant roaring when on a de-worming diet. Like the Himalayan black bears Rupert and Mary, he was eventually offered a new home at Butlin's holiday camp, Skegness, following an appeal on the BBC television programme Panorama.

61 *Right*. With the Rivers Stour and Avon and two or three of the latter's tributaries all within five miles of Ferndown, angling has naturally been a popular pastime locally. George Slaughter caught this salmon in the Avon at Ringwood.

62 The Ferndown golf clubhouse, built in 1922 and pictured here *c*.1937. The club's professional in those pre-war years was Percy Alliss, one of the biggest names in the game. His son Peter, who was brought up in Ferndown, is best-known as a golf commentator on television.

63 The first tee and clubhouse at Ferndown Golf Club showing post-war additions, including a verandah and glazing to the lounge. The club and neighbouring *Dormy Hotel* have hosted many major tournaments including the Hennessy Cup in 1982 and 1984, and the Ladies European Professional and British Open events in 1987 and 1989 respectively. In his autobiography, Peter Alliss writes: 'Lovely Ferndown, seven miles north of Bournemouth, in the heather and pine country which I adore, in what must be one of the most mellow corners of England.'

Churches and Schools

64 The entrance to Holy Cross Abbey at Stapehill, which was a Cistercian nunnery for almost 200 years.

65 Inside the Chapel of Our Lady of Delours at Holy Cross Abbey, Stapehill. The chapel, built between 1847 and 1851, has two naves, one for the nuns, who never mixed with the public, the other for the congregation.

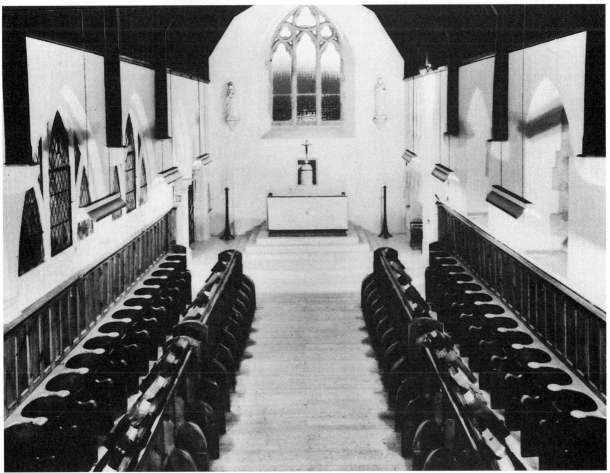

66 Another view of Holy Cross Abbey showing the cabbage patch cultivated by the nuns, who also kept bees and grew hay.

67 The Presbytery at Holy Cross Abbey, Stapehill. Since the nuns left in 1990, the abbey has become a flourishing craft centre with gardens and historical attractions.

68 All Saints Church, Hampreston, was originally a chapel of Wimborne Minster. The tower, chancel and one or two other features are 14th-century but, like so many other churches, the building underwent a major reconstruction in the 1890s.

69 The interior of All Saints Church showing the 'lofty chancel arch', as Hutchins describes it.

70 The original Ferndown Congregational Chapel in Victoria Road, which stood at the corner of what is now Westwood Avenue. It was destroyed in 1905 by a fire thought to have been caused by a firework on bonfire night. The building which replaced it was the present United Reformed Church in Wimborne Road.

71 The Sunday school class at the Victoria Road Congregational Chapel shortly before it was burnt down. The whiskered gentleman is the church superintendent Charles Roe, who later became Ferndown's scoutmaster and was also the local rates collector. The boy on the far right is farmer's son Mark Brown, who went on to become a well-known Ferndown character.

72 *Above*. The Primitive Methodist Chapel which adjoined Galton's Stores and Post Office at the corner of Wimborne Road and Victoria Road, Ferndown. The chapel building has changed little in appearance in the intervening 70 or 80 years but is now a pine furniture store.

73 *Right*. Lady Wimborne lays the foundation stone for the Ferndown Methodist Chapel, built on the corner of New Road and Ringwood Road on land which she had donated.

74 *Above left*. The fore-runner of the present St Mary's Church, pictured *c*.1901. It doubled as the Ferndown Infants School and was later the Church Hall.

75 *Above*. The present St Mary's Church soon after it was built in 1933 on land donated by Mrs. Lyon, who lived nearby in Dudsbury Avenue and was determined to prevent the building of a pub on the site. She also left money in her will for a tower to be added and this was built in 1969.

76 *Left*. Members of the St Mary's Church Choir on an outing to Weymouth in Mr. Robertson's of Longham charabanc.

77 *Above left.* Members of the St Mary's Church Girls' Friendly Society in 1937. They are Millie and Ada Dean, Ida Brown, Helen Harding, Barbara ? and Mrs. Spreckley, the wife of the rector.

78 *Left.* The Congregational Church at Longham, built in 1841 at the junction of Ham Lane (leading away to the left) and Ringwood Road. The same junction today is one of the busiest in the area but the church survives as the United Reformed Church.

79 *Above.* Victorian pupils at Hampreston village school pose for the camera. The school, opened in 1875, is the building with the tall chimney.

80 *Left.* Ferndown's first teacher Teresa Trevett pictured with her infant charges outside the original church infants school, *c.*1901.

81 *Below left.* Ferndown County Council School, opened in 1915 and described in a Press report at the time as being 'surrounded by spacious playgrounds' and 'thoroughly up-to-date in structure, having every appliance for carrying on the work'. It was demolished in 1990.

82 *Below.* The staff at Ferndown School, *c.*1929, including the long-serving Mrs. Trevett (seated, second right). The full line-up is thought to be (*back row, left to right*) pupil teacher Miss Vi Bracher, Mr. Flower, Miss Patten and *(front)* Miss Keeping, Miss Hannay, Mr. Bowering, Mrs. Trevett, ...?

83 A class at Ferndown School, probably photographed on the same day as the teachers (*c.*1929), since Miss Keeping and Miss Bracher (right and far right) are both wearing the same clothing. The pupils include, in the second row from the back, gipsy twins Reuben and Caleb Wareham, whose rock and roll hairdos were about 40 years ahead of their time!

84 Pupils at work at the Manor House School in Ringwood Road, Ferndown, *c.*1946, including (front row, third from left) Helen Tyler (née Slaughter) who, with her husband Geoff, lent many of the pictures for this book. She recalls that a bomb dropped outside the school early in the Second World War. The private school between Penny's Hill and Woodside Road was formerly the home of Edward Cheeseman.

Transport Old and New

85 Len and Billy Moors, who called themselves 'The People's Butcher', pictured with their delivery cart in 1922. Their shop was a large wooden shed at Hilltop in Wimborne Road.

86 The horse-drawn delivery wagon of oil and hardware merchants Fred Morris and Sons, whose shop was in Victoria Road, Ferndown.

87 *Left*. More horse-drawn deliveries, this time from brothers Roy and Bill King, from Home Farm Dairy in Ringwood Road, Ferndown.

88 *Below left*. A later form of delivery wagon in the form of Alan Dean's Deansbury Produce van. The location is the corner of Wimborne Road and Ameysford Road, Ferndown, *c*.1955.

89 *Below*. Also from the 1950s is this shot of Albert Bolton with his delivery van. Bolton's Dairies is one of the few pre-war companies which have survived to this day.

90 *Above.* Station Road, West Moors, showing the level crossing, railway station and (far left) the *Railway Hotel*, now the *Tap and Railway*. West Moors was also the station for Ferndown.

91 *Left.* Q class 0-6-0 locomotive number 30546 approaches West Moors station before its closure in 1964. The line continued for some years to take fuel trains as far as the army petroleum centre on the edge of West Moors.

92 *Below.* Uddens Crossing, pictured in 1964 and showing the Uddens Estate siding on the right and the points of the Uddens Abattoir towards the left. The siding was laid in 1943 to serve a Government depot and was in use again for the abattoir from 1953-65.

93 *Top left.* The so-called 'Ferndown Road Bridge', which crossed the River Stour in New Road, West Parley. It was built in 1910 but collapsed a few years later and was replaced in 1923 by the present New Road Bridge.

94 *Middle left.* Five traction engines testing the New Road Bridge following its construction in 1923. The bridge provided Ferndown and West Parley with a more direct route to Bournemouth. The combined weight of the five traction engines, supplied by Mark Loader, who built most of Bournemouth's early roads, was 60 tons. The test was obviously effective as the bridge is still in use today.

95 *Bottom left.* A more distant view of the New Road Bridge, taken soon after its construction in 1923.

96 *Below.* Ferndown contractor Ernie Jolliffe and his gang, pictured with their steam engine at Bear Cross. Jolliffe surfaced some of the roads in Ferndown and surrounding villages.

97 *Left*. This restored steam engine, photographed in the 1950s, originally belonged to Jim Hutchins, of the A31 Café, Ferndown, whose name and address are painted on the side. The transport café—also known as Jack's Cabin—stood near the site of the present-day McDonald's restaurant. The wartime owner was murdered by an American serviceman from the U.S. military hospital at St Leonards.

98 *Below*. Harold Soffe's garage in Ringwood Road, pictured here in the 1920s, specialised in cycle repairs.

99 *Above*. Three potential customers for Mr. Soffe, namely sisters Ella, Nora and Lena Elton, who lived in Church Road. The date is 1925, when (aside from walking) the bicycle was still the most popular form of personal transport for the majority of people, not to say the only affordable form.

100 *Left*. Looking towards Penny's Hill crossroads in the early 1930s showing a sprinkling of cars along Ringwood Road. A bicycle shop is among the businesses which now occupy the Redline Garage site (left of picture).

101 *Below*. The view looking down Victoria Road from the centre of Ferndown in the early 1950s showing the Victoria Garage on the right. The garage was founded in 1929 by Charles Cobb and Albert Haskett, who in 1931 were advertising 'repairs and complete overhauls' and 'any make of car or motor cycle supplied'. The garage was sold to Mick Whalley in 1947.

102 The Ferndown by-pass cuts a swathe through the countryside during construction in 1985. Towards the bottom of the picture, West Moors Road snakes towards the village of West Moors (out of the picture on the right) and Ferndown (left). A little way beyond the top of the picture (also just out of shot) is the Ferndown Industrial Estate. The road relieved Ferndown of much of the pressure it used to suffer, though the remaining traffic could hardly be described as light.

Moments in History

103 This was the scene at Stapehill in January 1913 after the gable end of a cottage on the Oakfield Estate collapsed, killing 73-year-old widow Harriet White and 11-year-old Nellie Hinton. Witnesses at the inquest said Mrs. White had repeatedly complained about the state of the cottage since the demolition of an adjoining slaughterhouse. The collapse involved 15 tons of rubble and the victims, who were in bed at the time, were dead by the time the debris was removed. The inquest jury criticised the owners of the house and the local authority for failing to condemn it.

104 Staff at the Red Cross Hospital in Pinewood Road, Ferndown, during the First World War. The hospital occupied a house known as The Hut and treated men of senior rank. (The lower ranks went to a chapel next to Galton's Stores in nearby Wimborne Road.) The house, which belonged to a Mr. Rose, a tea planter from India, later became St Mary's Vicarage but has since been demolished.

105 *Left*. First World War veterans and other ex-service personnel on parade for the opening of the British Legion Hall in Church Road, Ferndown, by Sir Richard Glyn in 1934.

106 *Below left*. Children in fancy dress process along Albert Road, Ferndown, during the coronation celebrations for King George VI in 1937.

107 *Below*. Children and a few mums and grandparents gather on land at Penrose Road, Ferndown, to celebrate V.E. Day in 1945.

108 A band of Royal Navy cadets marches through Penny's Hill during the 1963 Ferndown Festival procession.

109 It's Operation Ferndown Festival for members of the Chamber of Trade as they pass the Cosy Café in Ringwood Road during the 1963 procession.

110 Members of the Wimborne and Cranborne Rural Fire Brigade in the late 1940s. The Ferndown firefighters include Station Officer Bob Chick (middle row, sixth left), Mike Lewis (middle row, far right) and Alf Higbee (front row, far left).

111 In 1953 a heath fire on Ferndown Common destroyed Ferndown's fire engine. Ironically, the firemen who lost their brand new engine on the heath were also the winners of the county pump competition in the same year! The winning team included (back row, left to right) Mike Lewis, Alan Dean, Charlie Hiscock, Horace Higbee and (front row) Charlie Heywood, Ken Webb and Roy King.

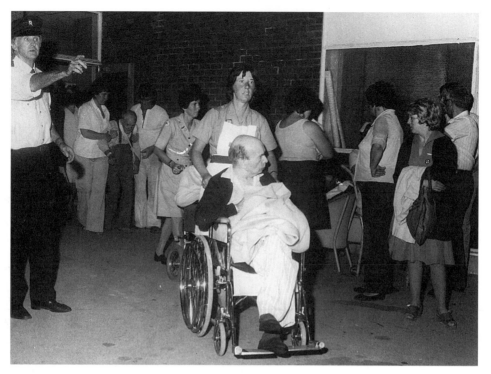

112 The summer of 1976 produced the worst drought in living memory and led to heath and forest fires on a grand scale. This photograph by Simon Rowley was taken at Ferndown Upper School as geriatric patients arrived following the evacuation of St Leonards Hospital. All 320 patients were evacuated as flames swept through the forest between Matchams and St Leonards, although in the event the hospital buildings survived unscathed.

113 One of the worst fires in 1976 swept through trees and undergrowth in the grounds of the army petroleum depot at West Moors, raising public fears of a major explosion. Rows of petrol jerrycans can be seen (left and centre) in this picture by Simon Rowley as smoke blackens the sky.

Ferndown People

114 Dorset's most successful smuggler Isaac Gulliver, pictured in old age. He dominated the contraband trade in the Ferndown area and for many miles around towards the end of the 18th century.

115 Isaac Gulliver's wife, Elizabeth, who came from Sixpenny Handley. She bore the smuggler a son and two daughters.

116 Hillamsland Farm, Longham, where the Gullivers lived from 1778 until about 1782. The part-Jacobean farmhouse next to Dudsbury golf course still has a huge cellar and, like many other local properties associated with smugglers, is reputed to have a tunnel leading to cottages at nearby Dudsbury. Another building connected to the Gullivers is Gulliver's Farm at West Moors. The brick-built barn is said to be the oldest building in West Moors.

117 Smuggler's Cottage in Wimborne Road, Ferndown, in 1965. The building is said to be 400 years old, which makes it the oldest in Ferndown by a long way. Its timbers are believed to have come from the timbers of a Spanish galleon wrecked on the Dorset coast. For much of its history Smuggler's Cottage was the only dwelling on this part of the heath and in the 18th and 19th centuries it was a popular haunt of smugglers, who often passed this way on their way inland from the coast. The cottage suffered serious fire damage in the mid-1980s but was soon repaired to resume its rôle as a tea room and bed and breakfast establishment.

118 John Prior, who worked at Stewart's Nurseries and is here seen wearing the Horticultural Society medal awarded for his work with fir trees.

119 Albert Bolton, of Bolton's Dairies, another company still in operation today.

120 Marine John May and his wife, who lived at Hilltop, Ferndown. John was a hardy individual who, whatever the weather, used to strip down each day to wash using water drawn from the well at the bottom of his garden.

121 James Stone, a gamekeeper on Lord Malmesbury's estate at Hurn Court, was also a travelling preacher who spread the gospel around the villages. He lived in Church Road, Ferndown.

122 Harry Hobbs, another of Lord Malmesbury's gamekeepers, who had some of his 'victims' preserved and kept them in glass cases above the fireplace.

123 Ferndown farmer Mark Brown, pictured in the uniform of the 6th Dorsets in 1916. He was injured later that year on the day after his best friend was killed. Many years later, he sold a large slice of land between Church Road and Victoria Road for development as one of Ferndown's first private housing estates.

124 Not a scene from *What's My Line?* but the Baker brothers, Fred (who worked for Fey's butcher's shop in Wimborne Road), Jim (who worked for Stewart's Nurseries), and Bill (Sutton's the grocery store and bakery at Longham).

125 Mary Ann Shiner, who counted them in and counted them out. Born in 1871, her nursing duties in Ferndown over many years included delivering babies and laying out the dead. This picture was taken in 1934.

126 Sisters Nora, Lena and Ella Elton pictured outside their home in Church Road at the junction of what is now Westwood Avenue. Their parents Charlotte and Charles had a market garden and grew the first tomatoes in Ferndown.

127 George Luther with his pony and trap outside his home at Longham. The Luther family were poultry dealers.

128 Poultry keeper Daniel Wilcox and his wife Frances, who kept chickens on the wasteground now occupied by St Mary's Church, Ferndown, before 1930.

129 Ferndown farm labourer and strong man Syd Kensington, who could lift a five-gallon barrel of liquid from the ground with one hand (although on this occasion he appears to be using two!).

130 Helen Slaughter, seen here in the 1940s with Ferndown's most popular four-legged character, Fanny the donkey. Fanny was owned by the artist Gerald Summers, who lived at Green Worlds, Tricketts Cross. Fanny, who was loved by everyone, was primarily a pet but also worked for her keep, pulling a trap and a garden cart and also hauling logs from Ringwood during a coal strike. Gerald Summers' friends included one of the leading artists of the day, Augustus John, who lived locally and was a regular visitor.

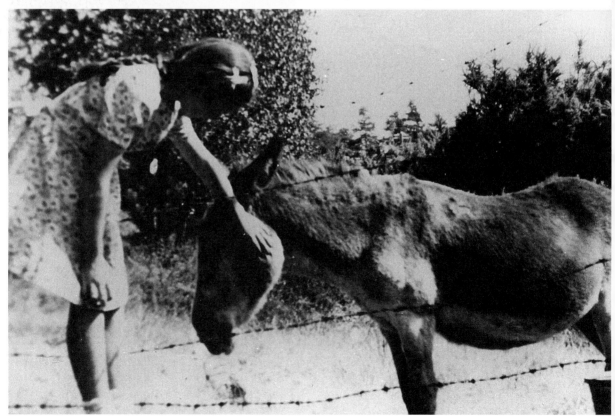

Wimborne Road

131 An early 20th-century view of Wimborne Road looking west and showing the entrance to the Stewart family home on the right. Tricketts Cross is a little way behind the photographer.

132 Ferndown Hill House, home of the Stewart family, whose Victorian market garden business has grown into two major garden centres today.

133 *Above*. The view along Wimborne Road, *c*.1900, showing the junction with Victoria Road on the left and the Manor Dairy (later Bolton's Dairy) in the background.

134 *Right*. The caption over-printed on the postcard may identify this as Ringwood Road but it is in fact Wimborne Road, *c*.1925, looking from a point opposite the junction with Victoria Road towards Tricketts Cross. The buildings include the Post Office (far right) and the Mission Hall next door. Between them is a sign advertising 'Ghrimes and Champion, auctioneers and valuers'.

135 *Above right*. A rare shot of Wimborne Road looking towards Tricketts Cross from a spot almost opposite Bolton's Dairy.

136 *Above*. Looking along Wimborne Road from the junction with Victoria Road towards the corner of Church Road, *c*.1920. The woman on the bicycle is passing Goswell's Garage.

137 *Left*. Wimborne Road looking towards the corner of Victoria Road (right) and Tricketts Cross, *c*.1950.

138 *Right*. Somewhere in Wimborne Road, Ferndown, possibly between the junctions of Victoria Road and Church Road, *c*.1908.

139 A horse waits patiently with its cart at the corner of Beaufoys Road, *c.*1908.

140 The Ferndown by-pass runs across this site today but in the 1930s, when this picture was taken, it was the Woolslope waterlily beds off West Moors Road. Nearby was Mr. Joseph's nudist colony and local character Percy Christopher remembers crawling through the surrounding undergrowth with his friends for a sneeky look!

Victoria and New Roads
and Dudsbury Avenue

141 Few pictures do more than this one to illustrate the extent of Ferndown's transformation since the turn of the century. The photographer was standing in what is now Queens Road and looking across Wimborne Road and straight down Victoria Road. Only two or three buildings are in sight, including Galton's Post Office and Stores (far left) at the corner of Wimborne Road and Victoria Road.

142 & 143 Two views of Victoria Road looking towards Wimborne Road. The horse droppings in the foreground of one picture and the cyclist and horse and cart in the other suggest that both were taken before the internal combustion engine began to make its presence felt in the 1920s.

144 Victoria Road in the 1940s looking towards Wimborne Road.

145 An unusual view of New Road, Ferndown, looking towards Parley Cross.

146 Dudsbury Avenue in the 1920s.

147 The view along Dudsbury Avenue from Ringwood Road in the 1930s. Note the rustic bus shelter.

Church and Albert Roads

148 Church Road looking towards Wimborne Road. The entrance to the Ferndown Council School can just be seen on the left. Note the cycling delivery man with his enormous basket.

149 A slightly later picture, taken from the other side of Church Road and a little further back, showing the school gate on the right of the picture and part of the school buildings on the left.

150 Church Road in the 1920s with the wall of the old St Mary's Church on the right. In those days when children could walk to school in the middle of what is now one of the busiest roads in Ferndown.

151 The view along Church Road showing on the right the site where St Mary's Church was later to be built. The land was then used as a chicken run.

152 A similar view after 1933, showing the new church on the right, before the addition of a tower.

153 The view along Albert Road from Victoria Road, *c.*1908.

154 Albert Road looking from the Church Road end, *c.*1920, is one of the closest residential streets to Ferndown town centre. The road was named after Queen Victoria's husband, Prince Albert.

Tricketts Cross and Ringwood Road

155 Unrecognisable today is this view of Tricketts Cross in the 1920s looking along the road to Ringwood. Today's busy Tricketts Cross roundabout would be towards the left of the picture. The cottage is above the site of the present-day *Smuggler's Haunt*.

156 Believe it or not, this leafy lane is now the busy Ringwood Road, but seen here in the 1920s when viewed from Tricketts Cross looking towards St Leonards.

157 *Left*. Ringwood Road looking towards Penny's Hill from Tricketts Cross, *c*.1925. The area around the crossroads acquired the name Penny's Hill from Mrs. Emma Penny, who ran a laundry there towards the end of the 19th century.

158 *Below*. Penny's Hill from the west, *c*.1925. The large signboard (centre) directs visitors to Ferndown Golf Club. The parade of shops on the right dates from 1895.

159 *Above*. Looking west across the Penny's Hill crossroads in the 1930s. The RAC man can just be seen directing traffic in the centre. To the left is the Methodist Chapel, now the fire station.

160 Penny's Hill looking east in the 1930s with the AA man taking his share of traffic duty. The AA box can just be seen outside the garage on the corner of Victoria Road and Ringwood Road (left).

161 Penny's Hill in the 1940s showing Turner's pharmacy on the right. This shop remained a chemist's until January 1997, when it became Ferndown Post Office.

162 Looking west across Penny's Hill in the 1950s.

163 Ringwood Road, Ferndown, *c*.1904. The exact location is uncertain but is probably on the western side of Penny's Hill.

164 The view from the corner of Church Road (left) and Ringwood Road looking towards Penny's Hill, *c*.1925. The land to the left of the direction sign was later bought for the building of St Mary's Church.

165 Looking along Ringwood Road towards Penny's Hill from an almost identical spot, *c.*1950. Church Road is on the left and Dudsbury Avenue leads off to the right.

166 Ringwood Road between Ferndown and Longham, *c.*1920.

Stapehill, Hampreston
and Longham

167 The crossroads at Uddens looking towards Ferndown, *c.*1925. The road to the left ran up to Uddens House and the one to the right went through to Ham Lane. Notice the lone milkchurn on the corner now occupied by the frontage of the *Old Thatch* pub and restaurant.

168 Uddens House, built in 1747 and demolished in 1955, was the seat of the Greathead family for much of this period. The picture dates from 1938. Uddens is first referred to as 'Uddings' in the 10th century and probably derives from a Saxon who settled there.

169 *Above.* Stapehill Post Office (far left) and adjoining houses in Wimborne Road West in the 1950s. The Post Office still operates at the same building.

170 Hampreston village at the turn of the century. The building with the tall white chimney in the middle distance is the village school.

171 *Below*. The Vicarage, Hampreston, in the 1930s. It was demolished after sustaining bomb damage during the Second World War.

172 *Above right*. Manor Farm, Hampreston, home of the Trehane family and (right) Rose Cottage, *c*.1930.

173 *Below right*. Hampreston village in the 1930s.

174 *Left*. Ham Lane, Longham, in the 1930s, when it was known as Hampreston Lane.

175 *Below left*. A steam-powered lorry puffs its way through Longham at the turn of the century.

176 *Below*. The 'smithy' at Longham Bridge, run for many years by the Cherrett family, who were also involved in smuggling. The last blacksmith was Harry Gray.

177 *Above*. The village pond at Longham, long since filled in, and on the left, Lady Wimborne Cottages. A story is told of the day Longham blacksmith Neddie Cozens threw a gipsy into the pond for mistreating his horse.

178 *Left*. Longham Bridge with the Longham Mill in the background. The bridge, built by John Wagg, of Ringwood, in 1728, carries a metal plate warning that anyone damaging the structure will be guilty of felony and liable to transportation for life.

179 *Below*. Longham House, home of Miss Selina Bush and her parents, Admiral and Lady Bush, since about 1900. The family are descended from Oliver Cromwell.

The View from Dudsbury looking towards Longham. H.S.

180 Local writer, artist and archaeologist Heywood Sumner's distinctive drawing of the view across the Stour valley looking from Dudsbury towards Longham, *c.*1921. Longham Mill is the building in the distance (right) with the tall chimney.

181 The view from Dudsbury Hill looking down Christchurch Road towards Parley Cross.

Bibliography

Original Sources
Hampreston Parish Register, Dorset Record Office
Settlement affidavit by William Lockyer (1812)

Published Sources (Books and Booklets)
Ashley, Harry, *The Dorset Village Book* (1984)
Burden, Richard, and Gordon Le Pard, *A New View of Dorset* (1996)
Chilver, K.M., *The Vanished Village of East Parley* (1968)
Dacombe, M. (ed.), *Dorset Up Along and Down Along* (1935)
Davis, Brian, *Ferndown: The Back of Beyond* (1996)
Dayrell-Reed, T., *Shove Ha'penny* (1929)
Densham, W. & J. Ogle, *The Story of the Congregational Churches of Dorset* (1899)
Draper, Jo, *Dorset: The Complete Guide* (1986)
Greenhalgh, Audrey, *Ferndown. A Look Back* (1991)
Greenhalgh, Audrey, *Along Longham* (1990)
Guttridge, Roger, *Dorset Smugglers* (1984)
Hutchins, John, *History and Antiquities of the County of Dorset*, third edition (1861-70)
James, Jude, *Wimborne Minster: The History of a Country Town* (1982)
Kelly's *Directories of Dorset* (1902, 1911, 1920, 1931)
Mills, A.D., *Dorset Place-Names* (1986)
Mills, A.D., *The Place-Names of Dorset*, Part 2 (1980)
Mills, A.D. (ed.), *The Dorset Lay Subsidy Roll of 1332* (1971)
Mitchell, Vic, and Keith Smith, *Branch Lines Around Wimborne* (1992)
Morris, John (ed.), *Domesday Book: Dorset* (1983)
Price, Geoff (ed.), *Rectors and Patrons of Hampreston* (church leaflet, revised edition 1993)
Rumble, Alexander R. (ed.), *The Dorset Lay Subsidy Roll of 1327* (1980)
Stoate, T.L. (ed.), *Dorset Tudor Muster Rolls* (1978)
Stoate, T.L. (ed.), *Dorset Tudor Subsidies 1523-1593* (1982)

Published Sources (Periodicals)
Christopher, Percy, 'Curiosities of Ferndown', *The Dorset Magazine* (Dorset Life), September 1994
Bournemouth Daily Echo, 'Ferndown Lion, Bears Go to Holiday Camp', 6 December 1955
Guttridge, Roger, 'Toiling Nuns at Stapehill', *Evening Echo* (Bournemouth), 21 January 1993
Guttridge, Roger, 'Travels of Rich Smuggler Gulliver Linked to Parish', *Evening Echo* (Bournemouth), 29 August 1996
Guttridge, Roger, 'Readers Shed Light on Smuggler's Home', *Evening Echo* (Bournemouth), 5 September 1996
Illingworth, Alan, 'Caring for Ferndown's Past', *The Dorset Magazine* (Dorset Life)

Index